On The Origin Of Paranormal Species

AMY LAURENS

OTHER WORKS

SANCTUARY SERIES
Where Shadows Rise
Through Roads Between
When Worlds Collide
The Complete Sanctuary Series

KADITEOS SERIES
How Not To Acquire A Castle

STORM FOXES SERIES
A Fox Of Storms And Starlight
A Stag Of Snow And Memory

SHORTER WORKS
April Showers
Bones Of The Sea
Darkness And Good
Dreaming Of Forests
It All Changes Now
Of Sea Foam And Blood
Rush Job
The Ice Cream Crown Skating Races
Trust Issues

NON-FICTION
How To Plan A Pinterest-Worthy Party
On The Origin Of Paranormal Species
The 32 Worst Mistakes People Make About Dogs

INKPRINT WRITERS SERIES
How To Write Dogs
How To Theme
How To Create Cultures
How To Create Life
How To Map

Find other works by the author at www.amylaurens.com/books.

AMY LAURENS

AUSTRALIA

'Vampires: Blood, Seduction and Social Acceptance Throughout History' originally published in *Aurealis* #137, Feb. 2021.
'Werewolves: Liminality, Power and Transformation Throughout History' originally published in *Aurealis* #143, Aug. 2021.
'Mermaids: Desire, Longing and Death Throughout History' originally published in *Aurealis* #136, Nov. 2020.
'Fairies: Malevolence, Beneficence and Nature Throughout History' originally published in *Aurealis* #139, Apr. 2021.
'Unicorns: Strength, Freedom and Awe Throughout History' originally published in *Aurealis* #141, Jun. 2021.
'Dragons: World Origins, Evil and Knowledge Throughout History' originally published in *Aurealis* #145, Oct. 2021.
'Goblins: Greed, Anti-Semitism and Neurodivergence Throughout History' originally published in *Aurealis* #146, Nov. 2021.

Trade Paperback ISBN: 978-1-922434-39-5
Case Laminate ISBN: 978-1-922434-97-5
eBook ISBN: 9798215691861
www.inkprintpress.com

National Library of Australia Cataloguing-in-Publication Data
Laurens, Amy 1985 –
On The Origin Of Paranormal Species
106p. cm.
ISBN: 978-1-922434-39-5
Inkprint Press, Canberra, Australia
1. Literary Criticism—Fairy Tales, Folk Tales, Legends & Mythology
2. Reference—Signs & Symbols

First Edition: July 2023

Summary: An exploration of the symbolism of a variety of magical and mythical creatures throughout history.

CONTENTS

With thanks to Terry Wood at *Aurealis* for enabling the creation of this book, originally as a series of articles for the critically acclaimed *Aurealis* magazine. The articles have been lightly edited in this new iteration, but they wouldn't exist at all had not *Aurealis* agreed to take them on.

Written gratefully on the land of the Ngunnawal people, who have been telling their stories here for countless generations.

INTRODUCTION

Even before I was an English teacher and a writer, I was fascinated by the idea of truth in mythology, or truth in fairy tales. The ideas that there was some quintessential element of myths, legends and fairy tales that was *real*, that was *actual*, captivated me, and I spent long hours in the fairy tale section of my university library, pouring over books for no particular end.

I rather thought that if I were to do an Honours year, I'd like it to be on that topic... But I could never really coalesce in my head what a thesis on that might look like, and so I gave the idea away—forever, I'd thought, but fate had other plans.

It was Maggie Stiefvater and Krista Ball that brought the idea back to the forefront of my mind years later; Krista because, as a writing buddy, she persuaded me to pursue publication of my non-fiction in the first place, and Ms Stiefvater because she wrote online about the story behind her *Wolves Of Mercy Falls* series: she too was enchanted about the idea of the truth-in-the-myth, only she was after the *symbolic* truth, what these creatures meant, what they were used as a stand-in for. That, to her, was the fundamental point of such creatures in fiction—and I realised that if I was going to do anything particularly interesting with mythological creatures (to me; I'm not making any particular judgement about what does or does not interest other people), I too wanted to understand their symbolism, their historical meaning, so that I could grapple with what that might mean in a contemporary setting.

What would the contemporary equivalent be of an attempt to rationalise nature? Or death? Or the ocean? What would that *look* like?

In order to find out the answers, I had to begin at the beginning, and figure it out: what did these mythological creatures *mean*?

And so, dear reader, you have this book: an exploration of the symbolic meaning throughout history of seven mythological or paranormal creatures, chosen partly for their enduring popularity and partly for the degree to which I thought I might find something interesting in the research. Sometimes I was very fortunate, and those two categories overlapped.

I hope that within these pages, you too can find something that causes you to look anew at creatures you thought you knew, to understand them in a different light, sometimes more flattering, sometimes quite damning—but either way, most definitely more complex.

There's no denying that simplicity carries its own sense of satisfaction... But complexity is rich, and delicious, and food to grow on.

Enjoy, dear reader—I do hope you grow.

Amy Laurens, March 2022

VAMPIRES: BLOOD, SEDUCTION AND SOCIAL ACCEPTANCE

MENTION THE WORD 'VAMPIRE' AND A VERY SPECIFIC set of characteristics immediately spring to mind for the modern audience. While we all know authors and screenwriters who take liberties, nonetheless the basic suite of vampiric characteristics seems so familiar, so fundamental to their very nature, that it may be surprising to learn exactly how modern many of these apparently immutable conventions are.

In fact, there have been three distinct periods in the identity of the western vampire: the vampire of European folklore, particularly prevalent in eastern Europe; the first fictional vampires, created in the 1800s; and the contemporary version most readers will be familiar with.

Vampires reached the peak of their folkloric popularity from the mid-1600s through to the end of the 1700s, when fictional vampires began to take over. However, the folkloric vampire bears only a passing resemblance to the complex, more-than-human vampires of the twenty-first century.

Le Vampire, lithograph by R. de Moraine (1864).

Throughout eastern Europe in the seventeenth century, vampires gripped the public consciousness. These vampires were revenants, people returned from the dead as barely more than corpses. They were said to hunger for blood, specifically of their loved ones and close friends, and rose from their graves at night to feed from the living. Sudden spates of inexplicable deaths or illnesses were considered signs of vampiric activity, and towns took to the graveyards, digging up suspects until they found a corpse that fit the physical criteria of a vampire: a bloated belly; blood around the eyes, nose, and/or mouth; hair, teeth and/or nails that seemed to have grown; and a ruddy and apparently 'healthy' complexion, sometimes in stark contrast to the person's appearance in life.

This vampire apparent was then treated in a variety of ways to ensure that their dark shenanigans ended: they may have been staked (various woods were popular in different locations, with aspen being a common favourite), had their clothes pegged down to prevent them from rising, or most commonly, had something placed in their mouths to remove the vampiric curse. This token often took the form of a stone, a coin, or another piece of metal, often carved with religious incantations. Corpses were often buried with these tokens pre-emptively.

Alternately, a body was sometimes buried surrounded by sharp objects such as knives, so that if the corpse did awake with vampiric tendencies, it would puncture its swollen stomach on the sharp objects. Grains or other numerous small objects were sometimes also scattered around the gravesite, in the belief that vampires would stop to compulsively count the grains.

Of course, there are scientific explanations behind the characteristics of the corpses people took to be vampires. In his book *Vampires, Burial and Death*, Paul Barber elucidates the reasons behind these 'vampiric' appearances.

When bodies decay, they often fill with gases in the torso, causing the stomach to appear swollen or bloated. This gas can also put pressure on the circulatory systems of the body, causing blood to seep from the nose and/or mouth and the skin to seem ruddier, an effect particularly notable if the person was pale in life. If pressure is applied to the torso of this bloated body, the gases can be forced through the vocal cords or the bowels, causing the body to groan or fart. And as decomposition continues and fluids are lost, the tissues of the body shrink, exposing the roots of the teeth and nails, making them appear to have grown.

A link between vampirism and porphyria has been suggested; this has been largely rebuffed by the medical community, however. More convincing is a possible link between vampirism and rabies, which can lead to both light and taste/smell hypersensitivity (garlic, anyone?), disrupted sleep patterns, a compulsive drive to bite, and a bloody frothing mouth. Furthermore, rabies is carried by (among other animals) wolves and bats, both closely associated with vampirism.

Thus the scientific reasoning behind the folkloric vampires of the seventeenth and eighteenth centuries; but what of their symbolic meaning?

As ever, the fear of death is prominent in vampire symbolism here. The folkloric vampire is someone who has passed through death but has for some reason failed to have their soul continue on. Similar to ghosts, the vampire was presumed to cling to its mortal life, visiting the friends and family members its spirit still longed for. This easily represents a projection of the desires of the living: unable to accept the finality of their loved one's passing, they assumed that the loved one is similarly unaccepting.

The vampires of folklore thus represent a collective desire to hold onto our deceased loved ones, and a very human desire to supply supernatural reasons to explain phenomena that seems otherwise inexplicable.

It seems inevitable, then, given the archetypal nature of these representations, that—once the Empress Maria Theresa of Austria passed laws banning the exhumation of bodies for the purposes of desecrating them and other European countries followed suit, signalling the end of widespread belief in real vampires—vampires would transition from the realm of folklore to the related but distinct realm of fiction. Society may have been forced to give up on the notion of loved ones returning immediately post-death in the real world—but in fiction, everything is possible.

The first fictional vampire was Lord Ruthven, styled on none other than the poet Byron by his physician John Polidori in 1819. Here we begin to see the foundations of the modern vampire: Ruthven is mysterious, alluring, attractive, rich, and—unlike the vampires of eastern European folklore—unable to be killed. He spends his days seducing beautiful women, concocting somewhat elaborate plans to marry his notional-friend's sister, and then tearing out said women's throat in an ecstasy of cruelty.

Although there were a handful of subsequent vampires in fiction throughout the 1800s, a gap then occurred until, at the end of this century, the most iconic vampire of all time entered the stage: in 1897 Bram Stoker published *Dracula*, consolidating this new kind of fictive vampire forever through the eponymous protagonist, Count Dracula. Like Ruthven before him, Dracula is mysterious, handsome, charismatic and socially sanctified by his veneer of aristocratic wealth.

Undoubtedly, the modern reader will be familiar with most, if not all, of the defining characteristics of the Dracula-esque vampire: in addition to being rich, seductive and addicted to human blood, Dracula is endowed with the ability to make more of his own kind, as his bite is contagious. He possesses supernatural powers of strength, personal healing, telepathy, hypnotism, shapeshifting and teleportation, allegedly granted to him by the devil; can command animals and influence the weather (to an extent); sunlight functions as a kind of kryptonite, weakening his powers considerably; he is primal and predatory, pitying humans for their emotional weakness; is unable to cross running water except at high or low tide, as well as being unable to enter a dwelling uninvited; and is repelled, calmed, or ultimately destroyed by the usual anti-vampiric arsenal of garlic, crucifixes, holy bread or water, wild roses, and sacred bullets.

One might think, then, especially in our day-and-age, that such a character could only be construed as *more* than human—as *super*human. However, Stoker's novel makes it clear: Dracula, and others like him, are a concrete embodiment of metaphysical evil. Stoker's work makes it difficult for us to sympathise with the Count, not *despite* his superpowers, but rather *because* of them. Thus, the vampire is presented to us as *less* than human; a creature corrupted, parasitic and fundamentally exploitative of the best of human nature.

The symbolism of such a vampire is at least threefold.

Firstly, the with prevalence of tuberculosis and syphilis at the time, the idea of contagious demonic possession must have been tantalising as a fiction.

Secondly, the Victorian cultural investment in the Christian-esque supernatural meant that this physical embodiment of evil was a compelling figure not only in fiction, but also in moral and spiritual discourse. This is, of course, one of the strengths of the speculative fiction genres: the ability to essentialise difficult concepts into something concrete and tangible, so that we are better able to grapple with them. Indeed, Stoker himself notes in *Dracula* that it 'is only when a man feels himself face to face with … horrors that he can understand their true import.'

Thirdly, these early fictional vampires lend themselves almost incontestably to a Marxist reading: they are the elite, both physically because of their strength and socially because of their wealth, and they depend entirely on the parasitic exploitation of others, usually those of lower social standing, in order to survive. The parallel between this kind of vampire and the wealthy aristocrats of Victorian-era European society are clear—as is Stoker's condemnation of these vampiric aristocrats as less-than-human, able and yet unwilling to demonstrate compassion for others, particularly those on the margins of society.

Finally, then, we come to the late twentieth century and the birth of the modern vampire, largely thanks to urban fantasy author Anne Rice, who established a modern vampiric tradition carried on by the likes of Charlene Harris, Stephanie Meyer, and many others. As one would expect in the postmodern era, when cultural standards are up for negotiation (particularly if they are elitist) and pastiche is art, contemporary vampires vary widely in their traits.

However, they remain distinctly vampiric in their thirst for blood, their charisma, and their supernatural abilities (though these often vary). What distinguishes them most from their earlier fictional counterparts is their emotional complexity: where the Dracula-era vampire feels no compassion for his victims, the contemporary vampire is often fully cognisant of the moral ambiguity of their actions, sometimes even experiencing anguish over their need for blood to sustain themselves. They may still seek to placate their conscience with a variety of rationalisations, but the very fact that this rationalisation is needed proves the vampire's new self-awakening. They are no longer less than human, disinclined toward the best of human emotion, but are now *more* than human: a human being, amplified.

We can see then that, view through one lens, the quintessence of the fictional vampire has not changed over the centuries: they are still rich, seductive and exploitative. What has changed, however, is our attitude toward them. Instead of abhorring the wealthy one percent for the self-focused and usually exploitative nature of their wealth, we instead long to be them—or at least, be swept away by them, as the proliferation of contemporary vampire romances can attest: an interesting commentary on our acceptance of the exploitative systems in which we operate, in direct contrast to Stoker's denunciation thereof.

Optimistically, we could infer that this speaks to a cultural acceptance of class mobility as at least a theoretical possibility: we are not now the wealthy elite, but perhaps if one of them fell in love with us, we one day might be. Less optimistic is the alternative interpretation, whereby we have been successfully lulled by our oppressors into a false sense of security, a kind of communal Stockholm syndrome where we sympathise with the difficult moral decisions our economic overlords must make if they are to continue exploiting our labour successfully.

On the other hand, Rice herself has noted that many people from social and political minorities have found solace in her reinterpreted vampires because they see in them the struggle of the outsider. In reflecting on her own life experiences, Rice has drawn parallels between the struggles of her fictive vampires and her search for meaning outside of organised religion; thus, her vampires become symbolic of the everyperson's search for significance outside of the cultural systems they have been abandoned by.

These modern monsters are cognisant of their monstrousness (code not for objective monstrosity, but for attributes unacceptable to mainstream society) and yet refuse to yield to the notion that, because they are monstrous, they are therefore undeserving of love, dignity and fundamental rights. Thus, through this lens, we might see contemporary vampires as evidence of perhaps the kindest of all postmodern impulses: the desire for universal rights for all human beings.

Perhaps, then, in stark contrast to the exiled, alien vampire of folklore, the contemporary vampire is indeed a symbol of acceptance; a celebration of the hope that perhaps, if a creature such as this can find love and belonging, so too might any given human, regardless of the isolation society might attempt to enforce.

In a Guardian article in 1995, British Politician Andrew Roberts famously noted that the 'liberal believes that a man, once stripped of his national and cultural identity, will become everyman—citizen of the world. The conservative knows that, in fact, he will become bewildered, schizophrenic, unhappy and lonely.' Regardless of one's personal political leanings, it is certainly very interesting to note that as the world grows incrementally more progressive in its embrace of universal human rights, so too do our vampires transition slowly from creatures bewildered, unhappy and lonely, to cultured citizens of the world.

Whether this is the frightening symptom of a widespread cultural Stockholm syndrome wherein we imbue the most exploitative tier of society with empathy and nuance, or whether it is more comfortingly symbolic of our search for belonging in an increasingly fragmented world where we are all confronted with our own monstrosity on a regular basis, it seems certain that vampires, with their connections to the enduring human preoccupations of death, attraction and acceptance will maintain their popularity for decades to come.

WEREWOLVES: LIMINALITY, POWER AND TRANSFORMATION

Author's note: This article almost exclusively explores the symbolism of the Continental European werewolf and its descendants, leaving aside for the time being shapeshifters from other cultures and continents.

WITH A HISTORY EVEN FARTHER-REACHING THAN that of vampires, werewolves are perhaps the ultimate paranormal creature. While there are stories of shapeshifters in practically every culture on every continent, the werewolf, as a specific subset of shapeshifter, has endured in fame and popularity throughout literal millennia. But why is this? What is it about the notion of a human transforming into a wolf that has long fascinated us, giving this mythical creature life enough to endure throughout the ages?

The answer lies, of course, in the symbolic significance of the werewolf, in what it has to offer culture as a metaphor for some of our more abstract concerns. And, as any concept that has endured for so long, the werewolf has maintained its position of symbolic importance by flexibly transforming to suit the most pressing concerns of society in each period of its existence.

Historic references to werewolves extend back as far as the Epic of Gilgamesh, in which a woman transforms her ex-lover into a wolf. However, it is not necessarily implied herein that the man ever transforms back into a human; likewise, in the well-known Greek myth of Lycaon, a king of Arcadia who tested Zeus's patience (in the most common version of the myth) by serving him human flesh to eat, and as punishment was turned into a wolf. It is somewhat ironic that this king-turned-wolf ended up giving his name to a person who can transform into a wolf and back into a human again (a lycanthrope) when he himself was condemned to life as a wolf ever after.

Lycaon transformed into a Wolf (Hendrik Goltzius, 1589)

A much more satisfying origin for the werewolf, sufficiently recognisable to a modern audience as to deserve the name, can be found in the Nordic Saga of the Volsungs, wherein a father-and-son duo find a pair of wolf pelts that grant the wearer the ability to turn into wolves for ten days. In events also recognisable to a modern audience, the father and son go on a vicious rampage which ends only when the father fatally wounds his own son (whose life is spared thanks to otherworldly intervention).

Interestingly, throughout various parts of Europe during the 1500-1600s, a variety of people either claimed to be or were accused of being werewolves. Partly, these cases can be attributed to a small handful of facts: wolves were the most significant predator in Europe during that time period, posing a genuine threat to the livelihood of humans and livestock encroaching on their territory; scientific understanding had not yet disproved the ability to transform from human to wolf; religious fervour meant that supernatural explanations were favoured; and a handful of notable serial killers throughout history who claimed to be were-wolves themselves, either because they thought it might excuse their behaviour, or else because they suffered some form of lycanthropy, a rare medical condition in which people genuinely believe they are shapeshifting into a wolf (or other creature) despite sensory evidence to the contrary.

(There are a handful of other conditions relevant to the belief in werewolves, but here we remain more concerned with the meaning of werewolves than their origins per se.)

In addition to this, madness in general has long been associated with the full moon (contemporary studies into this phenomenon are yet to demonstrate anything more than an anecdotal link, but the anecdotal link persists—ask any service-oriented professsional, including workers in emergency departments). Lunar imagery, of course, has permeated werewolf folklore for centuries, strengthening this link between werewolfism at madness.

Intriguingly, the full moon is a regular-but-comparatively-infrequent occurrence just like werewolfism, coming only once every twenty-eight days—and therefore begging the question, in the absence of any notable female werewolves in history: is werewolfism a kind of stand-in for male menstruation, a regular period of heightened emotion and hormonal surges that lead to perceived unpredictability and instability?

The moon, with its continual but ever-changing presence, points another key aspect of werewolfism throughout history: its liminality.

In most folkloric traditions, humans transform into wolves in liminal spaces, which is to say spaces that are neither entirely one thing nor entirely the other. The location of the transformation echoes the transformational nature of the act itself, being a place that is neither here or there, neither this nor that. For example, Eastern European folklore often has werewolves transforming under a fence, a literal symbol of the transition from human-controlled land to wilderness. Other traditions set the transformation in the pigsty, the structure on a farm farthest from the home and thus once again existing on that liminal boundary between domesticity and untamedness. Still other traditions place the transformation in the forest itself, a symbol of the human shedding their 'civilised' self in favour of the forest wild, whether willingly or not. Regardless, these liminal settings all underscore a fundamental characteristic of the werewolf: that it is neither fully human, nor fully animal, always present but, in its form, never fully resolved—just like the moon.

There is one other context wherein much of Christianised Europe would have been familiar with the concept of neither fully human nor fully other during this time, and that is in the figure of Jesus Christ. However, to suggest that werewolves occupied the same sacred space of 'not fully human' as Jesus was obviously unthinkable; thus, werewolves posed a serious religious problem during the sixteenth and seventeenth centuries, given that much of the population accepted their existence as fact.

Two explanations for werewolves were posed. One was that God was the only being capable of true transformation, and thus werewolves used sorcerer-like powers to create the *illusion* of turning into a wolf; the other was that, despite official church doctrine to the contrary, the devil could also somehow enact transformation. It was the latter that captured popular imagination: for people at the time, it was clear that werewolves, with their neither-fully-this and neither-fully-that nature, could only come about via one underlying source: a pact with the devil. Thus, the liminal setting of the werewolf's transformation was an apt metaphor for the uneasy liminality of the werewolf itself: Not only did it raise questions of human vs. animal, domestic vs. wild, it also raised questions about whether it was *civilised*, both as an antonym of 'wilderness' but also in the colonial-religious sense of Christian, right, moral, and superior.

Thus, the connection between the werewolf and moral depravity was cemented, the werewolf themselves the picture of a 'lost soul', either because they had willingly made a pact with the devil (as was presumed with serial killers) or else because they had done wrong and been cursed therewith as punishment. This symbolism was underscored for the people of the time by the connection to the wolf, a creature widely regarded as behaving excessively and immorally, and a nod to the symbolism of the New Testament which often refers to Christians as sheep and threats to them as wolves.

Of course, the liminality of the werewolf sat just

as uncomfortably with the irreligious as with the religious at this time: not only were wolves considered natural enemies of humans, but the inability to characterise werewolves accurately placed them outside the natural hierarchies of dominance that were believed to exist (eg Aristotle's scala naturae, or the Great Chain of Being). This discomfort with creatures, concepts and persons that defy categorisation continues today; postmodernism has done much to advance western society beyond a strictly binary interpretation of the world, but the social preference for things to be either-or, this-not-that, remains.

Perhaps one of the clearest aspects of werewolf symbolism, however, relates to control. The transformation from human to wolf is, to the historic eye, an inevitable decline from rationality into base emotion and impulse, from moral obligation to immoral impulse. The werewolf's transformation, therefore, and their subsequent violence, functions as a symbol of a traditionally masculine (though socially deviant) reaction to loss of control: either the individual is cursed to lose control of themselves and is thus given over to violent and often sexual impulses; or else the individual *chooses* to cede control, or chooses werewolfism as a form of power in response to a lack of perceived power in other aspects of their life. At a loss for healthier coping mechanisms to deal with feelings of helplessness and rage, the man gives up on rationality and is controlled by his temper and base urges, accepting raw physical power as a substitute for actual effective control.

This metaphor is at its most poignant through a Marxist lens: the individual, usually male, usually from a blue-collar or working-middle-class background (a counterpoint to the aristocratic vampire), is unable to exert control over their lives in a way that is meaningful to them, having primarily only access to physical power and restricted (if any) access to abstract forms of power such as wealth, authority, and so forth. Thus disempowered and disenfranchised, our protagonist stumbles upon an object or makes a deal with the devil that will enable them to transform into a wolf—the ultimate nature-motif of physical power throughout most of continental Europe prior to urbanisation. The wolf, being the ultimate creature of power, allows the man to exact revenge upon those who would keep him from his rightful state, i.e. that of having sufficient agency over his own life. Thus balance, in our protagonist's eyes, is restored.

Of course, there is a divide in werewolf mythology that is relevant at this point, namely the extent to which the werewolf is cognisant of their own actions. While some folkloric traditions have the werewolf fully self-aware during their time as a wolf (thus underscoring the immoral nature of the literal murder and pillaging that may occur), other traditions maintain that the shift to wolf from human often comes as an uncontrollable surprise for the individual. This split roughly equates to whether or not a physical item is donned in order to transform into a wolf, with the deliberate putting-on of such an item implying that the individual will retain a sense of self-awareness while a wolf.

The alternative is a trope most werewolf fans will be familiar with: the individual who arrives back at self-awareness with gaping holes in their memory (and, frequently, their clothes), nothing but contextual clues to hint at what they have done as horror gradually dawns on them, coupled with regret, self-loathing and terror. In this instance, the individual has gained power but without control, and thus the transformation, instead of improving their situation, makes it worse. For this metaphor to have a happy ending, the werewolf must learn control, either by avoiding triggers or actively altering triggering events (avoiding the moon, taking a counter-active potion, locking themselves away, etc) or else by learning to exert mental and emotional control when the throes of the transformation come over them.

This particular aspect has become more and more popular as the werewolf has aged and matured: in our postmodern, postcolonial society where intersectional feminism is no longer a closeted, questionable philosophy, some degree of emotional intelligence is expected of everyone, regardless of background and gender. Even the Hulk has meditative techniques designed to enable him to exert a degree of control over his transformation—and so the idea of a creature that transforms uncontrollably in the face of overwhelming emotion has been shifted from the mainstream to the domain of the young adult, where this exact reaction remains both natural and expected as a young person transitions from child to adult, dealing with the surges and fluctuations in hormones that arrive as a consequence along the way.

Indeed, it is here that the werewolf finds a particularly apt symbolic home in contemporary times: what better place for a metaphor of physical change, loss of control, awakening of previously unexperienced urges and impulses, and at times overwhelming surges of emotion than during adolescence?

It makes sense that in a pre-Romantic, pre-Modernist world, this 'descent' into impulse would be considered a negative: western history, founded as it is on Greco-Roman values of logic and 'civilisation', has long preferred reason to emotion and logic to instinct. In this context, humanity has long been considered the benchmark for rational behaviour, and as we can see clearly from the layers of the werewolf symbolism, the descent back into nature is closely correlated with a descent into Hell. Nature is, of course, something first to be tamed (see: most of western history) and, even when the cultural zeitgeist transitioned to begin valuing emotion in the

Romantic period, nature is to be *bettered*, not simply appreciated.

Thus, it is unsurprising that it was only after the Industrial Revolution, somewhere around about the shift from Modernism to Postmodernism when nature began to be conceived of as valuable in its own right and worthy of preservation, that werewolf symbolism underwent its most significant shift. While even early werewolf films preserved the monstrous nature of these creatures, a confluence of social and technological factors meant that from approximately the 1980s onward, the werewolf began to accumulate layers of more positive symbolism:

- While historical-style werewolves undoubtedly still exist, the development of film technology meant werewolf films could actually *show* the transformation from human to wolf, inducing sympathy for an undoubtedly painful and startling transition;
- The postmodern predilection for pastiche allowed 'werewolf stories' to become backdrops for other genres, such as romance, thus broadening their appeal and making the creatures themselves less horrifying and monstrous;
- Increasing secularisation removed the 'soul' aspect from the werewolf symbolism, preferring instead to discuss 'consciousness' and freeing the werewolf from the threat of eternal damnation as a consequence of their existence;
- The rise of global capitalism, which thrives on

consumerism, actively encourages consumers to 'throw off' restraint, to act on impulse and instinct in order to consume more;

- Our ever-increasing awareness of humanity's impact on the climate and environment, coupled with a global shift toward urbanised living, weaves a longing for nature and an authentic connection to it through global modern culture, thus making the shift from human to wolf something symbolic of a return to 'purer' times;
- Globalisation exposes us to a wider range of 'ways of life', and the Other is slowly becoming less something to be feared and more something to learn from;
- And just prior to these cultural and technological shifts, the connection between werewolves—hairy, au naturel creatures who lived withdrawn from societal convention, shifting gradually from propriety to provocation—and hippies began this transition from outcast to counter-cultural icon.

In a post-colonial world, perhaps the pop-culture de-monstering of our monsters is inevitable.

Thus, fundamentally, the modern werewolf demonstrates the western shift toward self-reflection and emotional self-awareness. No longer is the werewolf a horrifying, monstrous Other; instead, it is a symbol of hope for all the people who live in the liminal spaces of society. If this beastly creature can find a home in the heart of millions, perhaps there is room there too for all those marginalised by dominant social paradigms, or for those whom society has long attempted to force into narrow, constricting roles. Perhaps we can learn to love liminality in the end.

Culturally, we have transitioned from a world where wolves are the scariest thing we can imagine to terrorise us at night to a world where the real villains are those who persecute the wolves for being different: humans, it seems, are scarier than wolves.

And yet, has this not ever been the case? It wasn't nature that frightened the villagers who believed wholeheartedly in werewolves, but rather something more than nature—humans becoming *more* than nature. Nature might be terrifying—but people, with the prejudices, ambitions and grievances, are infinitely more so.

Perhaps we were the real wolves all along.

MERMAIDS: DESIRE, LONGING AND DEATH

MEET A YOUNG GIRL RAISED IN WESTERN CULTURE AND chances are high that you've found someone who has, at least at one point in her life, harboured a love of mermaids. And it's not just young girls, despite them currently being mermaids' most commonly marketed-to demographic: throughout history, mermaids have held sufficient charm and appeal that they have maintained popularity throughout a host of cultural and political changes, across wide-flung geographical communities, and across age ranges.

From whence, then, do they draw their appeal?

'Appeal' is an apt word, because fundamental to the idea of a mermaid is that she is appealing—in direct contrast to many other popular paranormal creatures throughout history. Because in the 21st century there are sub-genres of romance exploring relationships with almost every paranormal creature imaginable, we forget that for most of history, many of these creatures were considered base, abominable, and often completely repulsive. The mermaid, however, holds the distinction of being perhaps the single most appealing of the paranormal species, at least in terms of the longevity of her appeal.

And so, it is with rather delicious irony that we explore the psychological symbolism and appeal of the mermaid: we are almost asking the question, what is the appeal of appeal? Why are we attracted to attractive things?

And as we will see, while there are some obvious answers to this question, there are some less overtly obvious (and thus, perhaps, more interesting) answers as well. First, however, it is helpful to establish the origin of the mermaid.

Every continent on Earth boasts some association with mermaids, from the selkies of Scotland and Orkney to Mama Wata, the great water spirit/s of Africa. Mostly, these beings are female (though there are sporadic references to mermen, notably in ancient Greek mythology). However, historically not all these creatures have looked the same, and although they may fulfil a similar role in society in terms of their symbolism, not all of them contributed to the pedigree of the modern mermaid.

There are, in fact, three distinct creatures that gradually merged together to form what we could recognise today as a 'mermaid'. Firstly, there are the Nereids of Greek mythology, who were sea nymphs depicted as beautiful, barefoot women belonging to Poseidon's court (although their parents were Nereus, the oldest son of the Titan Gaia, and Doris, daughter of the ocean Titan Oceanus).

Nereid riding a sea-bull (latter 2nd century BC).

Second are the sirens, dangerous temptresses whose primary job is to lure people to their deaths. Unlike mermaids, who have remained essentially consistent in their form since the medieval period, sirens have undergone many transformations. Originally conceived of by the Greeks as part-woman, part-bird creatures, it took many centuries for them to settle on their presently agreed-upon form, that of savage, attractive, dangerous part-woman, part-fish creatures that abide in the ocean.

Thirdly are water spirits in general, which take on a variety of forms and characteristics depending on their location. Mama Wata, for example, the great uber-water spirit found in many African cultures, had a reasonably variable appearance (often as a part-woman, part-snake creature, snakes in non-western cultures being considerably more revered than in cultures with a Judeo-Christian heritage). It was not until regular, consistent contact was established with Europe (both through the trading of goods and the European abduction of African people) that Mama Wata settled reliably into a recognisably "mermaid" form.

It was as the world became increasingly westernised that these diverse water women drew together to create the homogenous concept of the 'mermaid' we recognise today, taking on the beauty of the Greek Nereids, the allure and half-women, half-fish nature of the siren, and the power and ubiquity of the water spirit.

And so we arrive at the question: what is it that makes mermaids, these feminine water creatures with attractive feminine uppers and sleekly scaled fish lowers, so culturally powerful that they are able to not only captivate the humans who see them, but drag in a whole raft of other mythological beings to be subsumed into their species as well?

Let us start with their most obvious trait: their seductively beautiful appearance. Often glimpsed in the act of combing out their long, luscious hair, mermaids have clear links with feminine beauty and desire—so much so that, throughout the Middle Ages in Europe, the mermaid was used by the Church as a symbol for sexual immorality. Depictions of mermaids in religious artworks from this period almost exclusively represent her with both comb (symbolising pride in her physical appearance) and mirror (symbolising vanity, or an obsession with her appearance), and if a human is shown in her company it is to represent the human's fall from the 'straight and narrow' path of righteousness into the clutches of vanity, pride, and improper sexual desire.

Which segues neatly to the mermaid's second most obvious trait: sexual desire. Or at least, the sexual desirability of her *upper* half; what is the deal with the fish bits?

It is widely suggested in mermaid literature that a fish tail on a woman so overtly sexual and attractive can only be a symbolic stand-in for her unattainability. Lacking obvious female sexual organs, she is thus symbolic of a man's desire to engage sexually with a woman, only to be thwarted by the woman herself. She is the ultimate unobtainium. In this guise, she represents the frustrated longing of men at sea (whether literally or metaphorically) for intimacy, and the apparently fickle nature of women when it comes to delivering on the promises alluded to by their beauty: this type of patriarchal ideology believes that in the very act of daring to be beautiful, a woman is ipso facto making an offer to the viewing public, who gaze upon her not simply to appreciate her beauty, but with the clear expectation that that beauty will and ought to lead to sexual consummation. The mermaid, like other feminine subjects, are considered instead beautiful objects existing solely for male gratification—with the mermaid's tail and thus sexual inaccessibility symbolic of the frustration of men living under this paradigm who have their expectations thwarted when it turns out that beauty does not equal a promise after all. Seen with this patriarchal lens, the mermaid is longing, unrequited love, and heartbreak personified—equally applicable whether she is a vicious, tempting siren, luring men to their deaths, or an innocent romantic partner unaware that her chosen partner cannot survive in her aquatic world.

However.

While this may be a superficially satisfying interpretation (and a very common one), we can only assume that those who choose to interpret mermaids thusly are unfamiliar with creatures such as seals, whales and dolphins who, being mammals, engage in sexual reproduction despite their 'fish-shaped' lower halves and lack of externally visible reproductive organs. Let's just say that the above don't seem to prevent aquatic mammals from getting the job done, so as relationships go, the one between a ground-dwelling man and a sea-dwelling woman would be *complicated*, but hardly a physical impossibility.

So yes, the mermaid may represent thwarted sexual desire... but so do many other things. This does not sufficiently distinguish her as to justify the mermaid's immense and continuing popularity as a mythological being, especially in an increasingly intersectional feminist world.

However, there is a further complexity to consider that lends additional depth to this analysis. Those who have studied gender at any point may likely be familiar with the Virgin-Whore Dichotomy, a paradigm whereby women are assigned one or other of these roles as polar opposites on a linear spectrum.

What that means is this: either a woman is the sweet and innocence 'girl next door', pure, naïve, and nurturing, or else she is an object of desire, sexual, often objectified and stripped of any interiority, a force of nature both desirable and fearsome. Rarely—in media, in art, and, often in recent history, in life—is a woman permitted to possess traits from both ends of the spectrum. If a woman is a mother, she is not (in a western context) to be seen as an object of sexual desire. And if she is desirable, she cannot possibly be innocent, or at least cannot be allowed to maintain her innocence.

Mermaids bear obvious associations with the unfortunately named 'whore' side of the dichotomy, with their emphasis on sexual appeal. However, if this were their only defining feature, it would seem strange that a significant proportion of their fan base is young, pre-sexual girls. Either we have successfully indoctrinated young girls with the idea that their social value lies exclusively in their physical appearance, just as it does for the mermaid (an unfortunate but plausible possibility)—or for these girls, she must represent something else. For the sake of these girls, it would be nice to imagine an alternative symbolism.

So: the mermaid is beautiful, to be sure, and undoubtedly connected with appeal, desire and attraction... But her beauty seems intimately connected with something else intrinsic to the mermaid, something that humans, on the whole, lack: freedom. Freedom of movement, freedom of expression, freedom from the constraints demanded of women's bodies in above-ground lived communities. Yes, she is an object of male desire, but nevertheless, a mermaid may go where she chooses, do as she pleases. She is sexual, but she is empowered in this sexuality, unconstrained by modesty and able to exert power over those who would gaze upon her. And in addition to all of this, the myth of the mermaid is still permeated with a kind of child-like innocence, a sweetness and joy that sees her at home with flippant and charming dolphins, giggling in the waves in delight, ornamenting herself with starfish and shells, taking pleasure in the simple, tactile happiness of life.

And so, in the mermaid we see a feminine creature who is at once the innocent, nurturing girl-next-door, and the literal embodiment of autonomous sexual power. Rarely, in literature or mythology, do we get such a well-rounded feminine persona, permitted to be both the virgin *and* the whore. This is much a more satisfying symbol to pass on to our daughters.

But of course, there is even more to this paranormal creature whose popularity boasts a longevity outstripping that of almost every other paranormal creature. As well as sexual attraction, there is *another* fundamental aspect of the human experience that fascinates us to which the mermaid bears links: death.

As sailors have been known to leap from the boat into stormy seas at the sight of beautiful mermaids, fascinated by their Otherness and simultaneous familiarity, so humans have long been intrigued by death. Both familiar and fundamentally Other, death is an inevitability that is at once the ultimate danger, and at the same time in many contexts alluring. As humans, we always crave knowledge that is forbidden to us, and here the mermaid, with her beauty and danger, her paradoxical familiarity and air of mystique, is an apt symbol of death and whatever may or may not come after—especially in connection with sirens, whose sole reason for being is to lure unwary sailors to their fatal end.

So, the mermaid can be a symbol of desire, and a symbol of death. Apt, for a two-part creature to boast a two-part symbolism. But just as the mermaid herself unites two apparently opposing parts in one unified whole, so is there a theory about the mermaid's symbolism that unites these two facets of death and desire.

What else is there, integral to the mermaid myth, that also consumes sailors with both death and desire? Why, the sea, of course, with its two aspects: one alluring and desirable, calling humanity onward and over the horizon just as a mermaid attracts humans—and one cruel and capricious, threatening (if not delivering) a fatal end... just like a siren. Thus mermaids and thus the ocean, a very suitable symbolism given the influence of the Greek Nereids, daughters of the great Titans of the ocean itself, on the mermaid's evolution.

And we can take this symbolism one step further: the ocean itself is a common enough symbol for the birthing of new life, representative of a worldwide womb out of which life first arose—and what is life if not simultaneously alluring and desirable, and also cruel and callous?

Thus, at her heart, the mermaid is nothing more or less than a symbol of *life*: at once a source of attraction and longing and vitality... but also inextricably enmeshed with death.

This is a satisfying conclusion as to the enduring popularity of the mermaid. She is the primal, quintessential symbol of life and at the same time its two inevitabilities: our drive toward reproduction through sexual attraction, and our awareness of the inevitability of death that dogs our every footstep.

Whatever your preferred interpretation of her symbolism, it is doubtless that the mermaid has endured in popularity for centuries in part due to the flexibility of her interpretations. In the concept of the mermaid, it seems that there is something for everyone, and so it seems probable that her popularity is ensured for as long as the foreseeable future.

FAIRIES: MALEVOLENCE, BENEFICENCE AND NATURE

Author's note: For the sake of clarity, this article will proceed with the term 'fairy' to mean the Victorian-period being: tiny, butterfly-bewinged creatures that adorn many a (stereotypically feminine, often-pink) décor item. The term 'fey' or 'neo-fey' will refer to fairies depicted as essentially human in form and size. Thus, we shall progress from fey, to fairy, to neo-fey, the latter of whom also share cultural real estate with fairies in the contemporary period; and they shall all be grouped together under the term 'faerie'. This nomenclature is entirely specific to this article to avoid confusion therein and is not reflective of actual historical usage.

REGARDLESS OF WHETHER YOU DEFINE FAERIES NARrowly, as the supernatural beings associated primarily with early Celtic beliefs, or whether you define them broadly, encompassing a wide variety of supernatural nature-linked beings, one thing is certain: faeries are enduringly popular. Engendering both fear and awe in their believers, since early times faeries have been both a source of blessing and an unpredictable, capricious authority in need of appeasement. They have made a mark on human culture that has cemented them as one of the most beloved nonhuman creatures in all folklore and mythology.

But why is this? And what does our pervasive attachment to faeries really mean?

In order to uncover this, it is useful to take a brief tour through the history of faerie belief. There are three distinct periods in faery belief and popularity: the Celtic period, which influenced beliefs so significantly that they remained largely unchanged for many centuries; the Victorian period, which saw the faery (and many of their fellows) stripped of danger and authority; and the contemporary period, which sees a mixing of the two broad types of faeries.

Firstly, let us consider the fey and their cultural significance. Originating predominantly from British and Irish religious mythology with a helping of Scandinavian elves, these fey are powerful, tricksy, and fickle. It is relatively likely that, in the British Isles at least, the fey of common folklore arose as the gods and goddesses of the Celtic religions were displaced by Christianity in the early centuries of the Common Era.

Reflective of these pagan-religious origins, the early fey were tightly linked with both with nature in general, and with specific places (many of the deities of Celtic religion being genii locorum, or highly localised deities tied to a specific place). The fey were a ready symbol for the capriciousness of a natural world that often seemed hostile to humanity. Thus, from the beginning of the Common Era right through to the 1800s, the fey were often held responsible from everything from soured milk to illnesses (particularly tuberculosis), from series of unlucky events that might befall an individual to behaviours (particularly in children) that, in more contemporary times, might be considered signs of neurodivergence or symptoms of mental health conditions.

Of course, in this early period of faerie lore, when Christianity (among other factors) had demoted these beings from Celtic deities to something more akin to nature spirits (albeit often powerful ones), benevolent fey existed too. Hobgoblins, for example, were household beings that assisted with many chores—provided one did not acknowledge them, regardless of whether such an acknowledgement was favourable or not.

However, more commonly—and certainly so after the blurring of faerie lore with early to middle-period Christianity, wherein the fey were often reconciled to this new religious paradigm by being assigned the role of moderately fallen angel, too wicked for Heaven and yet not wicked enough for Hell—the fey were cast in a negative light, often depicted as taking pleasure in playing with humans as cats do with mice, capturing and enslaving humans as pets and oddities for their own amusement, and perhaps to torture.

Thus, the dominant attitude was that the fey were to be avoided at all cost. People who sought them deliberately ran the risk of entrapment in the land of Fairy or else of madness (or of both), and many beliefs centred around protection from the fey's malevolent exploits. Thus we have inherited such ideas as iron being a natural deterrent to the fey, as well as daisies, church bells (although particularly in Scotland, where the fey were separated into the more malevolent Unseelie and the less malevolent, possibly benevolent Seelie, church bells often protected one only against the worst of the fey), and hanging horseshoes open-end-up for protection (this is where the belief in horseshoes as lucky comes from, possibly because of their iron content).

'Fairy circles' also originate from this broad period, being usually either a ring of stones (small or large) or else a ring of mushrooms or toadstools, often ringing a particularly green patch of grass. Fungi fairy circles have a fascinating biological explanation: what appears to be a series of separate and distinct fungi arranged coincidentally in a ring is actually a single fungus, connected by literally miles of virtually microscopic 'roots', known as mycelium. This single organism throws up fruiting bodies at the tips of the outermost mycelium, resulting in a ring of mushrooms. The grass inside can be greener than outside the ring as the types of fungi that can create such rings are most likely to thrive where an old tree stump or perhaps an animal carcass provide a source of nutrition; as this source breaks down, no longer visible to the casual human eye, it enriches the ground around it, allowing the grass to grow more lushly at the same time as nurturing the fungi.

This biological explanation, though, does not detract from the connection between fey and these fungi circles. Rather, it cements the connection, pointing to the very heart of fey symbolism: just as these circles are a place where death is transformed into new life in the process of decomposition that drives the entirety of the natural world, so too are the fey seen to have an intimate connection with the natural world, with preserving its order, and with dispensing violence (read: death and decay) while simultaneously possessing a sense of wonder, awe, and beauty.

This being the case, it is at least superficially difficult to view the Victorian-era fairy as much more than an empty whimsy. Although the faerie-centric beliefs of this next era (loosely encompassing the 1800s and the early part of the 1900s) preserve the sense of wonder and beauty that permeated beliefs about the earlier fey, like many myths and stories during the Victorian period, much of their symbolic depth seems flattened. No longer capricious representations of nature, faeries in the Victorian era became harmless, sanitised, and thoroughly 'suitable for children'.

This, naturally, resulted in a paradigmatic shift: whereas the fey were the purview of all ages, Victorian fairies became the domain of children.

Of course, upon closer examination this does not by necessity diminish their symbolic power: These moderated fairies are indeed quite representative of their era, speaking to the social repression and strict social mores and strictures of the time. In the Victorian period, public behaviour at least was highly codified, with many of the grimmer or simply more *physical* aspects of life swept from the public stage as 'impolite' or 'inappropriate'. This is evidenced not only in the transformation of fey to fairies, but also in the changes to many of our most famous European-rooted fairy tales, with, for example, Cinderella's stepsisters transitioning from chopping off their toes and heels to fit into the shoe to the less gruesome variant we are more familiar with today.

Additionally, the Victorian era is characterised by widespread emerging industrialisation. Whereas once nature was the court in which human lives were weighed, the transition to industry saw swathes of humanity urbanised. No longer bound to nature's fickle whims, instead the people of this era were ruled much more determinatively by the whims of their factory masters. Humanity no longer required symbols of nature in the same manner as earlier

Take the Fair Face of Woman, and Gently Suspending, With Butterflies, Flowers, and Jewels Attending, Thus Your Fairy is Made of Most Beautiful Things – painting by Sophie Gengembre Anderson (1869)

populations; rather, people in this era could reflect upon nature with nostalgia and longing—and thus, although the roots of the apparently diminished fairies may lie in a desire to censure and censor, in actual fact we see that they reflect the culture around them no less complexly than did the earlier fey. These physically smaller, equally magical creatures reconnected with their benevolent sides and acquired butterfly or dragonfly wings, developing into symbols of wonder and the inherent magic of nature—a concept made all the more appealing by the revival of social interest in early Celtic history during Queen Victoria's reign. This evolution of appearance speaks to the first part of the faerie's appeal: that they can represent flexibly humanity's complex and evolving relationship with nature.

Before moving on to the modern era, let us momentarily step sideways and a little back to the fairy godmother, barely a concept before Perrault popularised the fairy tales of Cinderella and Sleeping Beauty in the 1600s. The fairy godmother is fascinating, for here is a fey creature in a time when fey were largely considered malevolent who nevertheless is characterised by her particular benevolence toward a human in need of help. How can this be so?

It is in the tale of Sleeping Beauty that we see most clearly the fairy godmother's roots: in this tale, the fairy godmother is not singular, but threefold. This triadic structure is reflective of many female deities throughout time periods and cultures in Europe, and is frequently linked to the concept of fate, something particularly demonstrated by the Greco-Roman and Eastern European Fates.

And it is not only their threefold existence that point to the Fates as the true progenitors of fairy godmothers: Fairy godmothers are characterised predominantly by their interest in human affairs, and by their benevolence and desire to advance the personal causes of their favoured human; likewise, the Fates were intimately concerned with the affairs of both humans and gods, though their interest was, perhaps, a little broader and more focused on holistic justice rather than advancing the cause of any individual in particular. In contrast, the fey were far less interested in the affairs of mortals except, at times, as sport.

Thus, a second source of the faerie's endurance in popular folklore: their inclusivity, in that they are able to sweep into their fold any number of other folkloric or mythical beings, who might otherwise have fallen by the wayside, emphasising the pliancy of the term 'fairy/faerie'.

So, what then, of the modern era, where Victorian-style fairies pervade the pinkified aisles of gendered toys and school stationery and make their almost-obligatory appearances in all manner of TV for children, while fey, or at least neo-fey (the often exoticised and sexualised version of the historic fey) permeate our fiction, both written and, increasingly, visual? What meaning can these beings, now so diverse as to practically represent different species, offer a modern audience to justify their continued popularity?

Of course, the answer is that faeries endure in modern society precisely because of those features that made them popular, useful symbols in the first place.

Firstly, faeries, both fey and fairy, maintain their connection to nature, often being tied to some form of elemental magic (as in the recent Netflix adaptation, *Fate: The Winx Saga* (2021), for example). And neo-fey frequently adhere to the rules established about the fey, avoiding iron, enjoying tricks and games, residing in a Fairyland which is both appealing and dangerous for humans, and dealing in enchantment and glamours. In this guise, they speak to that part of us that recognises that, despite our collective urbanisation, nature has the ultimate say. In a world where natural disasters are broadcast globally and climate change threatens our entire way of life, it seems clear that we still have need for fey that represent the most fickle, treacherous aspects of the natural world.

So too do we have use for the fairies, for the hope which they bring us and their gentle reminder that nature is magical, nurturing, awe-inspiring. Far from a simplistic children's motif, fairies connect us back to our innocent, child-like sense of wonder—and they do so often in the context of nature, inspiring us to connect, to wonder, and to care.

Secondly, in a pluralistic, postmodern society, it is unsurprising that multiple subspecies of faerie can happily coexist—a wonderful thing, that we should allow for such diversity even in our imaginary beings.

But more than this: like so many other mythological beings, faeries have become a potent symbol of the Other—and, as with many other beings, instead of fearing this Other, we seek to join them. Much could be made of this in terms of various social theories, but for the sake of brevity here let us confine ourselves to one final observation: if faeries have functioned throughout history as a symbol for nature, it follows logically that at least some of that function is preserved in modern society.

And thus, if we, despite the capriciousness of these faeries, still long to *be* them, well then, perhaps this is a glimmer of hope—that now, instead of objectifying nature as something to appease, we at once recognise its fickleness and the hold it has over our lives and *at the same time* seek to unify ourselves with it.

This, then, is the power of the faerie motif: our longing for and enchantment with the faerie symbolises our longing for and enchantment with the natural world. We may have trashed the environment, and climate change may be upon us, but the enduring popularity of the faerie points to the heart of humanity. And in that heart is hope: for nature is no longer something external to fear, but rather a culture we willingly desire to participate with.

UNICORNS: STRENGTH, FREEDOM AND AWE

Author's note: This article is less concerned with the origin of the unicorn so much as with its meaning; for a comprehensive and engaging exploration of the history of the unicorn, the author wholeheartedly recommends Chris Lavers' The Natural History of Unicorns *(2009).*

THE HISTORY OF THE UNICORN (IN THE GENERAL SENSE of an elusive, single-horned beast) has as many twists as the modern-day representations of its horn. For centuries believed to be a real creature, written about in non-fiction bestiaries and scientific literature, the eventual collective realisation that the unicorn as a distinct, naturally occurring species does not exist did little to dampen unicorn fever. If anything, the more evidence we have collected that the unicorn is a creature entirely invented by humanity, the deeper our collective obsession with it has become.

From certain small-pony TV shows to boardgames with particularly unstable beasts, from the stationery aisle at your local supermarket to any number of clothing outlets—both artist-designed and mass-produced—the unicorn is the ubiquitous imaginary creature of the 21st Century.

Why so? What magical, mysterious qualities does this one-horned beast possess that have sustained its popularity not only through time, but across cultures, continents, and through a literal 'extinction event' when all hope was finally ceded of finding such a beast in the wild?

The answer to these questions differs slightly across five key epochs of the unicorn's history, but nevertheless there are threads that tie them all together, threads of strength, freedom and awe that bind together this sparkling, multifarious beast. To unpack what this really means, it's time to trace the significance of the one-horned beast through the ages.

In the earliest period of our exploration, the unicorn is virtually unrecognisable as such. Encompassing the beliefs, myths, and scientific understanding of much of the Near East (Asia west of India) and the Subcontinent (India and other countries south of the Himalayas) prior to the fifth century BCE, unicorn-like representations were as diverse as they were integral. Sometimes appearing as scaled beasts and often distinctly bovine in appearance, these unicorns, these one-horned creatures, were less a species of their own and more a category of beast. Many of them are depicted in more-or-less two-dimensional friezes and paintings; some, particularly from the Subcontinent, are sculptures. It would be easy to dismiss the two-dimensional renderings as two-horned animals viewed from side-on, but the proliferation of uni-horned sculpture from this time and period makes this an unsatisfactory explanation.

Unicorn wall painting in Apadana, Shush, Iran.

But in order to see what is going on with these predominantly uni-cows, it is necessary to skip forward all the way to the 1930s, when one Franklin Dove (re)discovered a method for artificially creating unicornism in domestic cattle, allowing modern scholars for the first time a lens for understanding what the unicorns of the Ancient Near East might be depicting.

In the USA in 1933, Dove succeeded in surgically removing the horn buds of a young cow, leaving them attached via strips of skin (in order to ensure the horns wouldn't die), and then reinserting them centrally in the middle of the cow's forehead. As the cow grew, the horn buds fused together, resulting in a single, beautiful horn graduating from white to black to red.

It seems most plausible that the 'unicorns' depicted in the earliest representations are individuals demonstrating artificially induced unicornism. We know from the literature of the time that they are associated with strength, with leadership, and with royalty, and from what we understand of animal behaviour, this makes sense: the one-horned creature does indeed often become the leader of its herd, and subsequent to the 1930s (re)discovery of the horn-bud technique for artificially creating unicorns, animal behaviourists observed that a one-horned animal generally became the dominant animal in the herd (or flock), in much the same way as a hornless individual often becomes the dominant member in an otherwise dual-horned herd. The psychology behind this is beyond the scope of this article but accepting that this is indeed the case allows us now to parse the mono-horned creature of ancient Persia, India, Tibet, and other places in between.

By the 400s BCE, however, knowledge of this human-induced unicornism was not common—

whether it was 'no longer' common, or whether it had never been particularly common in the first place remains uncertain, but regardless, the Greek physician Ctesias was certainly unaware of it. Intriguingly, the association between unicorns and strength, however, persisted.

In the 390s BCE, after a long period in Persia as physician to the king, Ctesias wrote *Indica*, a book about 'India' (referring to modern-day Pakistan, the Himalayas and Tibet) that described the unicorn as a real, literal creature, originating somewhere in this 'India' region.

Ctesias's unicorn, which became the unicorn of popular culture at the time, was strong, wild, and virtually untameable, running faster than the fastest dogs and horses of the time and requiring packs of dogs and men with spears to bring it down, if ever it was captured. Ctesias colours his unicorn white, with a dark reddish head and a horn that is white at the base, black in the middle, and red at the tip (and interesting connection to Dove's artificial unicorn). He also provides a veritable host of biological features which implicate the Tibetan ass (the kiang), the yak, and the chiru (an antelope) as the source of facts fused together to make a one-horned legend (a veritable host of subsequent scholars have essentially ruled out the possibility that his description might be that of a rhinoceros, though as ever, historical uncertainty remains).

What is interesting, however, is that while Ctesias's unicorn was clearly a symbol of wilderness, being untameable and quintessentially unknowable, Ctesias is also the first record we have of unicorn horns being used as an antidote for and ward against poison. Drinking liquid from a unicorn-horn cup, Ctesias says, will protect the drinker from poison, convulsions, and possibly, depending on the translation, epilepsy.

There is documentation from this time period demonstrating that rhinoceros horns were used as drinking vessels. What is interesting, though, is that in the prior era, there are many myths and religious stories from the Persia-through-India region that involve a male nature spirit, often described as having a single horn (though not always), being first captivated and then captured by a human woman before being led off by her back to her civilisation, usually by her firm grip on said horn. While the underlying metaphor of the taming and civilising of nature are clear, it's also interesting to note that in many cases these nature spirits are associated with purification. To many of them is attributed the power to cleanse and purify water. Is it possible that Ctesias, in describing a 'real' creature of his time (if one with attributes amalgamated from three or four actual creatures), leaned a little too heavily on these myths, with which one can assume he was familiar, living as he did in Persia for many years?

If Ctesias did not, though, one can be certain that the next generation of unicorn enthusiasts did. Gradually, from about 100 CE to the late 1500s, the unicorn morphed from a one-horned ass with a horn that maybe could protect someone against poison if they drank from it, to pure white beast with a definitively magical horn (which may have fetched up to $100,000 modern equivalent on the market at the time, if you believe some translations) that played an integral role in both religious and romantic imagery.

In the earliest part of this period, the unicorn was a relatively solo stand-in for Jesus Christ, this not-necessarily obvious connection drawn in *Physiologus*, a book of animal stories presenting not only then-scientific information about the creatures therein, but also a Christian moral attached to each. It was in this era also that the earliest stories of male nature spirits (that also happened to often have one horn) being 'tamed' and introduced to civilisation by a woman had a contemporary resurgence—only, through the religious lens provided by the author of *Physiologus*, the story became an allegory for Jesus-the-deity being 'introduced to civilisation' (brought literally to Earth) because of a woman (Mary), though the parallels to the biblical story of Adam, Eve and the Fruit That Wrecked It All are also readily apparent.

Over the ensuing centuries, this allegory was fleshed out further, and around about 1100 CE unicorn artwork began to depict the woman and the unicorn with a variety of symbolic background characters that made this religious connection even clearer for audiences at the time.

However, the romantic and sexual implications of the earlier myths (one-horned man tamed by woman, who now leads him around by the horn, a suspiciously phallic appendage) were also obvious to anyone familiar with these myths.

And the readers familiar with these myths constituted an increasing section of the population as the stories grew in popularity, thanks to the sanction of the Christian Church. One can only assumed that the Church at this time was comprised either of people who found the dual symbolism helpful—the Bible contains many references, for example, to the church as the bride of Christ, and presents this as a template for a marriage relationship—or else people who naively assumed that the more erotic connotations would be buried by the religious ones.

Thus, by the time of the creation of the famous Verteuil Tapestries, around about 1500 CE, the unicorn possessed a dual symbolism: he is both a religious Christ-symbol, the embodiment of strength and awe willingly surrendering his own freedom; and he is the romantic suitor, 'captured' by the feminine wiles of his lover—and these threads of strength, freedom and awe are still alive and well in the symbolism of the unicorn today.

It is in this period too that the unicorn's horn consolidated its magical powers. Although Ctesias suggested that drinking from a unicorn horn could protect the drinker from all manner of ailments, it wasn't until circa 1100 CE that this belief became widespread, largely thanks to one Hildegard of Bingen, a German abbess who, it seems, based much of her work on the Islamic scientific writings of the prior few centuries, which evidence suggests were about rhinoceros horn. Exactly how the belief in magical healing and purification powers jumped sideways and became attached to 'unicorn horn' (often a narwhal tusk by this point, but also commonly walrus ivory) remains lost to history, but nevertheless the belief was persistent enough that it took some hundred years for 'unicorn horn' to be removed from common medical texts even after its effects (and existence!) were disproved in the early 1600s.

While this body of symbolism even now lingers in the aura of the unicorn, around about the 1700s, the religious aspect began to dim. Europe was entering, or preparing to enter, the Romantic Era, a reaction against the scientific reductionism of the Enlightenment, and the unicorn's symbolism shifted correlatively. This period, encompassing the 18th, 19th and early 20th centuries, is the peak era for unicorn hunting—hunting in the sense of tracking it down, for the unicorn was the 'cryptid extraordinaire' of the time, the ultimate symbol both of humanity's inability to entirely conquer nature—of nature's awe, and wonder, and mysteriousness—and also of the final frontier of nature, the final 'big discovery' out there and waiting.

It was during this period that the existence of the narwhal became more widely known; intriguingly, this had the opposite effect to that expected by a modern audience. Instead of adding to the evidence against the existence of unicorns, narwhals were seen as further proof that they must exist, as the prevailing western belief at the time was that the ocean was a perfect mirror of the land, and that all land creatures had an oceanic counterpart. Thus, if a narwhal existed, surely somewhere its land-dwelling mirror creature existed too.

Innumerable investigations were funded in this period, aiming to find and document a real live unicorn—and all failed, though only in the limited sense that they failed to find a unicorn, for indeed they were successful by many other measures, documenting and bringing to the world at large many other fascinating plants and creatures hitherto forth unknown to the global public.

And it was on the back of this, the final death throe of the unicorn-as-a-real-actual-beast, that Dove created his artificial unicorns in the 1930s, unlocking the mystery of the unicorn's symbolism in its earliest history. How nicely circular life sometimes is.

Of course, this brings us forward to the modern era of the unicorn! Now solidified as a horse-like beast with a single spiral horn, the unicorn is often associated with rainbows, themselves partly symbolic of all that remains mysterious and awe-inspiring in nature (despite our ability to explain them scientifically).

While there are still links to the idea of 'purity', the overwhelming symbolism is of something grand, magnificent, and out of the ordinary: a person who does not belong, but gloriously so. As with many other paranormal beings and beasts, the symbolism of the unicorn ends up being about belonging—or in this instance, about flagrantly embracing your own lack of belonging, everything that makes you unique and individual in the world. In this sense, the unicorn is still about strength—the strength to be one's self—and also about freedom: freedom from physics and biology in that it is a mythical creature, but also freedom from constraint, from social expectations, and from the mundanity of our lives.

Thus, despite the various twists and turns of the unicorn itself—in form, in nature, in origin—its symbolism throughout the ages has remained knitted together by those three threads: the unicorn as a symbol of strength, the unicorn as a symbol of freedom, and the unicorn as a symbol of awe. It is little wonder, then, that it has endured as the most popular mythic beastie of all time.

DRAGONS: WORLD ORIGINS, MORALITY AND KNOWLEDGE

LIKE MANY OTHER PARANORMAL OR MYTHOLOGICAL creatures, western dragons have three distinct periods in their history, with their symbolic meaning differing in each period. However, *unlike* many other creatures, the first two periods in the history of western dragons are lengthy and bear certain similarities in terms of the cultural role filled by the dragon. This means that up until relatively recently, the history of dragons in the western world remained quite consistent: dragons were a metaphor for evil, both external and internal, creatures to be either avoided or else slain at all costs.

Only with their migration into children's fiction at the very tail end of the 1890s did dragons undergo something of a rebirth, finding a new role as a charming, wise, and sometimes riddling children's companion. And, of course, once the adults saw this, they couldn't let the kids have all the fun!

But where *did* dragons come from in western culture? And what precipitated the shift in their symbolic significance—a shift all the more notable for its previous consistency?

In order to explore this effectively, let us start—of course—at the very beginning.

Dragons have a long-reaching history in terms of paranormal species in the west—if not *the* longest, certainly close to it. The first dragons are mentioned in early Norse mythology, in Ancient Greek mythology, in Ancient Babylonian creation stories, and in the Bible.

These early dragons boast three intriguing features.

One, their form is rather indeterminate, and is often connected to that of snakes. We see evidence of this in the word 'dragon' itself, harkening from the Ancient Greek drakon, or serpent (and closer scrutiny of the etymology suggests a further root, 'derk-', meaning 'to see'; hold that thought). The great Norse dragon is also called a serpent; early Latin bestiaries called the dragon 'the largest of all snakes'; and the Bible portrays Satan as a cunning, self-aware serpent who tempts humanity to sin and, as penance, must thenceforth slither on its belly in the dust, rather implying that, prior to this incident, the serpent had alternate means of transportation at its disposal—an implication supported by a variety of other sources that variously claimed dragons could swim, fly, breathe fire, and possibly were even venomous.

The second intriguing feature of these early dragons is that they are often related to either the beginning or end of the world, or its sustenance in between. Níðhǫggr is the Old Norse dragon who gnaws on the roots of the world tree (possibly chewing up the corpses of those considered by the Old Norse to be the worst of the worst: murderers, rapists and oathbreakers). Jörmungandr, the Midgard or World Serpent also of early Norse mythology, encircles the world, biting its own tail—when it eventually releases this grip, the end of the world as we know it will commence. Biblically speaking, the term 'dragon' is usually used to refer to Satan, either as a dragon at the end of times, or else as the serpent way back at the beginning. And Tiamat was the ancient dragon-goddess of the cosmos in Ancient Babylon whose death enabled the creation of our world. As we can see, there is not only a trend linking dragons with the fate of the world, but also a trend linking dragons with evil and/or destruction in these examples.

Thirdly, possibly because of this connection to the beginning and end of the world, these early dragons seem to often be associated with trees, usually trees with extraordinary powers: they are, perhaps, the symbol of the entire world and its 'aliveness', or else symbols for wisdom, or for wealth. Often, the dragon figure is depicted guarding this tree (as with Ladon, the dragon guarding the tree with the golden apples), in something of a symbiotic relationship with it (as with Níðhǫggr and Yggdrasil, the world tree), or else taking the role of the failed guardian, tempting humanity to commit wrong by means of the tree (Satan and the fruit from the tree of the knowledge of good and evil).

And so, despite the wide-ranging accounts of dragons during this long early period, there are overall generalities that can be claimed. Dragons are large, powerful, real creatures whose name probably relates to seeing. They are entwined with both the creation and the destruction of the world, and they guard (or fail to guard) sacred trees that impart life, wisdom and wealth—associations that dovetail neatly with the more metaphorical meaning of the verb 'to see': to understanding, to perceive intellectually, to envisage. The dragons of this first period, thus, are 'seers' in some way.

Moving forward, let us consider the middle period of western draconic folklore, spanning roughly the millennia from 1000 BCE to about 1900BCE. Here, we see that it was primarily the Christian dragon that endured with the greatest popularity, no doubt owing to the spread of the religion itself and the colonialism that tended to accompany this spread.

Thus, the dragons of this period are tightly linked with Satan or the devil and his character traits: dragons are a symbol of evil in the world, a monster demanding violence either in the form of sacrifices (see *George and The Dragon*) or else due to a reign of terror. For the people of the Middle Ages and

Renaissance, dragons symbolised greed (as seen in the character of Fáfnir, a man who *became* a dragon, so great was his avarice); they are creatures of excess, who overreach in the exertion of their power. Great predators, middle-period dragons hunted and pillaged and plagued, harassing and haranguing the common man until some great aristocrat trained in the fine art of dragon warfare could be conjured to slay the beast—the (supposed) power of a knightly education to vanquish evil, both literally and symbolically.

Saint George Killing the Dragon, woodcut by Albrecht Dürer (1501/4).

It is from this period that some of our most enduring dragon folklore derives: the damsel in distress kept prisoner by the evil, greedy dragon; the local tormentor who, like a malevolent god, reigns down terror from the skies and demands appeasing sacrifices (gold or people, either tend to suffice); the plated-armour knight, riding atop his chivalric steed with sword in hand to slay the beast holding the common people captive (either physically or as prisoners of fear); and of course, the ability of this great monster to breathe fire.

After all this negative press, it's little wonder that writers fell silent on the topic of dragons for a time, even as fantasy established a foothold as a 'real' genre and stories were filled with ghosts, fairies, merpeople and witches. It is likewise little wonder that it fell to children's writers, ever the vanguard of challenges to the mores of society, to revive the dragon conversation—nay, not simply to revive it, but to revitalise it.

One can never be quite sure to whom to attribute things such as these, but certainly Kenneth Grahame, of *The Wind in the Willows* fame, contributed significantly to the dialogue with his 1898 book *The Reluctant Dragon*; together with E Nesbit's *The Book of Dragons*, published in 1899, it marks one of the very first 'good' dragons seen in western literature.

Of course, as with any great transition, setbacks are inevitable, and for this particular setback the evidence is very clear about who to blame: one J. R. R. Tolkien, creator of Smaug, undoubtedly the most famous of his dragons, but also Glaurung (the father of Middle-Earth's dragons) and Ancalagon (reputedly the greatest of Middle-Earth's dragons). Tolkien's dragons are a direct call-back to the great dragons of the middle period: they are shrewd and mighty, evil, dangerous, fire-breathing, greedy for gold and sacrifice.

Thus it is that the third period for western dragon-lore didn't really find its footing until the 1960s, with the arrival of two worlds whose impact on the genre is as immeasurable as that of Middle-Earth itself: Pern and Earthsea.

In Pern, McCaffrey created dragons who were not only devoid of avarice and a thirst for violence and sacrifice, but who were actually *friends* with humankind, boasting telepathic bonds with their riders and actively working to the good of humanity. Alternatively, in the dragons of Earthsea (Ursula K. Le Guin) we find creatures still mighty and shrewd as the dragons of old, but instead of malevolent they are reserved and inscrutable, as far above the petty squabbles of humankind as the stars.

Together, these two worlds (introduced in 1967 and 1968 respectively) paved the way for the pedigree of dragons to come—and these days, it is commonplace to find any sort of dragon at all when you pick up a dragon-related story, from the capricious dragons of Westeros (who, of course, will allow a chosen few to ride and tame them) to the dangerous but also, quite frankly, adorable dragons of the popular *How To Train Your Dragon* franchise (also rideable and tameable by a subset of the population, albeit a much larger subset than that of the Westeros' dragons).

It is superficially tempting to suggest that dragons have become less one-dimensional, less absolute, for the same reason that many other paranormal and mythical creatures have undergone a similar transformation: in a postmodern world, ideological paradigms themselves are less absolute, and globally we have a better and more nuanced understanding of the range of cultural possibilities that fall within the scope we call 'human'—and there is a fair degree of influence from eastern cultures in the mellowing of western dragons.

Certainly, this predilection for cultural borrowing and a growing appreciation for monsters-with-a-conscience, for multi-dimensional villains, and for calling into question the whole nature of villainy and monstrosity themselves have not hurt the dragon. But the dragon underwent this transition somewhat earlier than the similar transformation of its mythical compatriots, the vampire and the werewolf, at the peak of modernism rather than riding with the rising wave of postmodernism.

In order to explore why this might be, it is useful

to ask at this point a summative question: what do all three of these periods of dragon-lore have in common?

Creative and destructive force, embodiment of evil, a scourge, a companion, a source of wisdom... Perhaps there are overtones of our relationship with nature in the transformation of the dragon as with the fairy and the unicorn, but a better unifying theory is this: it seems that fundamentally, the dragon—named for its ability to *see*—is a symbol of *knowledge*.

This ought not to be terribly shocking news for anyone who has been following along, associated as dragons often are with wisdom, ancient knowledge, and trees with the ability to impart an understanding of the concept of morality.

Whether that knowledge is considered good, evil, or even simply neutral, seems to be more reflective of the age the dragon lives in than any startling quality inherent in the concept of 'dragon' itself. Certainly, yes, dragons were for a significant period of history considered evil, but in a cultural climate where religion functioned in a primarily antagonistic manner toward science, is this any wonder?

The dragon moves from a period in which the knowledge handed down in stories was fundamentally concerned with the origins and future of the world (and thus is the dragon linked with guarding the wellbeing of either the world, or some other magically/religiously precious object) to a period in which the dominant western religion operated from an unfortunately (and often fatally) antagonistic paradigm toward the accrual of human knowledge (and thus is the dragon, or knowledge, depicted as the ultimate evil, threatening the morality of the Church and the upright individual, requiring an aristocrat to fulfil the priesthood function and banish the evil knowledge from the lives of the beleaguered peasants), and finally, to a new awakening at the height of the modern scientific revolution, where knowledge and its acquisition were no longer suspect, but were instead seen as the duty of humankind (c.f. Kennedy on the space program, that America's '*obligations*... require [them] to make this effort ... *for the good of all men*' [emphasis added]).

In this context, it is little wonder at all that the dragon, ancient wisdom and fearful knowledge, shifted from inscrutable external force to the antagonist, and from thence first to companion before, at last, claiming a role as protagonist.

One is only left to wonder, then, where the dragon will go from here. In an age of global warming and compassion fatigue, where global knowledge inundates us daily and more information is at our fingertips than ever before, what now becomes of this creature whose very value lies in its symbolic representation thereof?

Will the dragon soar to new heights as humanity pools its knowledge to conquer disease, hunger, climate change?

Or will it take flight once more as the scourge of the skies, a creature representing all the failures of humanity's hubris after we dared soar too close to the sun?

Only time will tell, of course—but I like to hope it will be the former.

After all, who doesn't love a 'good dragon' story?

Author's Postscript: It seems practically churlish to write an article linking dragons to world origins, morality and knowledge—even if the focus is western *dragons—without at least acknowledging the Rainbow Serpent, world-creator in many Aboriginal Australian religions; Quetzalcoatl, the great feathered serpent of the Aztecs who was, among other things, the god of learning and knowledge; and of course the great body of Chinese literature and folklore wherein dragons are powerful but largely benevolent, tasked with peace-keeping and rain-bringing, among other duties.*

It is interesting to note that these associations are consistent with the hypothesis that the dragon is a symbol of world origins and knowledge.

GOBLINS: GREED, ANTI-SEMITISM AND NEURODIVERGENCE

IN A SERIES ABOUT THE SYMBOLISM OF POPULAR paranormal and mythic creatures, it seems perhaps odd to include a piece on goblins. They lack the mystique of mermaid, the pervasive flexibility of the fairy, the ubiquitous charm of the unicorn and the allure of the vampire or werewolf. Television shows are not made about goblins; one does not peruse the stationery aisle at one's local outlet expecting to find goblin-themed notebooks or stickers. Barely anyone dresses up as them for Halloween or other cosplay events, and there is yet to be a movie or TV series focused around the adventures of a goblin main character. The reasons for this rest, of course, in the rather fraught history of the goblin. And yet, just in the last handful of years or so, the goblin is experiencing a resurgence—or, more properly, a rebirth, taking as it does the quintessential elements of the goblin and utterly repurposing them.

So what is this 'fraught history' of goblins? What are their quintessential features? And why, in our modern era, has this opened them up to such an intriguing rebirth?

While there is much contention about the meaning and origin of the word goblin—possibly via Old French in about 1195, maybe from Medieval Latin as early as 1140, or possibly even from Greek-by-way-of-German even earlier—by the time it became a commonly used signifier, the creature it referred to was well established. An other-worldly being akin to a sprite or early-period fairy (fey, in the nomenclature of this book), goblins were a category of mythical creature found throughout Europe.

(Many other cultures had similar beings, often translated into English as goblins; however, for the purposes of this article we shall constrain ourselves to their European origins.)

In places with overarching fairy/fey mythology, goblins were considered a subspecies thereof and, as with many other middle-European mythic creatures, their exact nature varied with geography. For the most part, goblins were considered a short, grotesque race of beings who specialised in trickery—as innocence as mere mischief, or as outrightly malicious as wanton murder and destruction.

In Anglo-Scottish folklore, the redcap is a short, stocky, murderous goblin with grisly hair and a red cap dyed thusly with the blood of its victims.

Hobgoblins (from the same region) were the friendliest incarnation of the goblin, being merely tricksters and, in pre-Christian times, actively helpful around the home.

Various Scandinavian fairy and folk tales feature

goblins, sometimes indistinguishable from trolls and sometimes alongside them.

Goblin illustration by John D. Batten from "English Fairy Tales" (19th century)

The trasgu or trasgo is a Spanish/Portuguese goblin of Celtic origin, a dark-skinned, green-eyed creature said to be both mischievous, nervous and proud, wearing either red clothes or clothes made of leaves depending on the region.

The Germanic kobold (considered the Germanic equivalent of a goblin, with the two words possibly sharing a common root) came in three forms, either as an ambivalent house sprite who only played tricks if insulted; an underground-dwelling creature similar to what we might now call a dwarf, but with a distinctly troublesome nature; and a sea-faring sprite that provided assistance to sailors. In all three cases, the kobold could be largely invisible, and could take on a variety of shapes and forms.

A final well-known example comes from the later part of this period in goblin history: the Erlking, introduced into German mythology in the late 1700s, via an earlier Danish ballad. Though more commonly considered an elf, he is also referred to sometimes as a goblin.

As well as their short stature and unappealing appearance, these early goblins also share similarities with others of the various fey creatures of the time: they were considered not to inhabit the mortal world entirely, being supernatural beings, and were often found in nature.

Thus, it might be tempting to write off these early goblins as mere reflections of nature, no more or less than their fairy counterparts, and leave the analysis at that.

However, we know that it is often ourselves that we best portray when we design, reflect on, or observe the supernatural, or indeed nature itself. Thus, the goblin can be considered a metaphor for the 'ugly' side of humanity: for greed, for selfishness, and for the deception and maliciousness these attitudes engender.

There is, however, an uglier side to the symbolism of these purportedly ugly creatures: racism generally, and anti-Semitism in particular.

The first recorded instance of racism in deliberate

connection with goblins is in Sir Walter Scott's 1830 book, *Letters on Demonology and Witchcraft*. In this, he creates a link between goblins—ugly, suspicious creatures with their connection to nature and their greed and murderous impulses—and the Sámi people, the indigenous population of large parts of Scandinavia and the adjacent Kola Peninsula in Russia.

In a similar vein, the links between goblins, with all their negative associations, and Jewish people has been, if not widespread, certainly visible for many centuries.

According to some scholarship, anti-Semitism was inherent in most European writing up until relatively recent times. This is not to suggest that every single European writer was vehemently anti-Jewish, but rather to note that, as cliches tend to do, cultural stereotypes of Jewish people both permeated and were promulgated by most of Europeans' writings for most of post-Christ history—and that these stereotypes were, by and large, negative, or at the very least unflattering.

From Shakespeare's greedy Shylock to the Nazi's propaganda posters, from early Christian church doctrine to contemporary groups like QAnon, these stereotypes of Jewish people have remained largely unchanged: a large nose, dark beady eyes and a swarthy frame; an abundance of hair, often red, often frizzy or tightly curled; a penchant for answering questions with questions; a greedy or miserly character and a suspicious, self-centred interest in financial matters; a tendency toward deception and shady business practices; and a thirst for illegitimately seized power that gives Jewish people star roles in many a conspiracy theory.

In contrast, there are relatively few Jewish stereotypes broadly propagated in western culture with positive associations, a proclivity for masterful violinery being perhaps the only common and incontestably positive cliche.

What is important to note, of course, is the distinct similarity between the list of goblin characteristics and the list of anti-Semitic ones. A race of people stereotyped as being short and ugly, with a lust for wealth, an untrustworthy disposition and a general dislike of or even hatred for (the rest of) humanity? While the relationship between goblins and Jewish people in literature broadly is certainly far from a one-to-one correlation, regardless the similarities are too numerous for comfort.

And, in fact, too similar for contemporary audiences to ignore: even mega-franchises such as Harry Potter have come under scrutiny this century for perpetuation of stereotypes that reinforce rather than diminish this correlation between goblins and Jewish people. Type the words 'goblin' and 'Jew' into any search engine, and the first several pages link to sites where people are trying variously to defend and condemn the franchise for the goblins it contains.

A quick summary: Rowling's goblins are short,

relatively ugly (by western standards) bankers with large noses, frizzy hair and an insular attitude. They are simultaneously oppressed by, and hold themselves as superior to, human wizards. And they lay claim to any object made by a goblin as forever theirs, demonstrating suspicion of anyone not goblin.

It is, of course, possible that Rowling was merely playing off goblin stereotypes in general; as previously noted, the list of characteristics is similar enough that any overlap may be innocent coincidence. One might have liked to think, however, that the film makers would have known better than to show Stars of David in the floor tiles at Gringotts, banking headquarters for goblins and the wizarding world at large. That, at least, seems too much to be asked to swallow as mere coincidence.

Thus, although the primary symbolism of goblins throughout the previous millennia is simply the darker side of humanity, there is an undeniable element of racism to them that has shaped their symbolism as well—significant enough that simple ignorance on the part of any hypothetical author is insufficient to excuse them from accusations of anti-Semitism.

Whether this anti-Semitic association is a 'second era' of goblin symbolism or simply an additional layer that has co-existed throughout the goblin's palimpsestory existence, there is perhaps insufficient proof to decide.

What is clear, however, is that goblins are experiencing somewhat of a revival in modern times.

Around 2018, 'goblincore' (also called 'goblin-punk') began, initially on Tumblr before spreading to Tik Tok and thence to other popular social media platforms. A term labelling a specific aesthetic and ethos, the movement really gained traction in late 2019, burgeoning into popularity in 2020 in part due to Covid-19-induced lockdowns which saw people returning to more traditional, 'cottagey' values and pursuits.

Indeed, goblincore is often described as the off-spring of so-called cottagecore: as an aesthetic gob-lincore emphasises nature (in particular the oft-ostracised aspects such as fungi, reptiles, amphi-bians, dirt, bugs—especially snails—decay, etc); the collection of 'shinies', or objects which are usually small, often physically shiny, and frequently items considered inconsequential or outright garbage to mainstream culture (e.g. rocks, bottle caps, nails or screws, odd-shaped twigs or leaves, feathers, sea-glass, small rusted items and so forth); and a devil-may-care attitude toward physical appearance that can vary from a healthy disregard for societal beauty standards to an outright lack of hygiene, though proponents can usually be found somewhere in the middle.

As an ethos, goblincore is founded in environ-mentalism (with a key focus on inclusive care for all parts of nature, especially the ugly and/or neglected ones, as a function of a holistic ecosystem), 'old-fashioned' cottage skills (such as sewing, gardening, preserving and herbalism), anti-consumerism (emphasising up-cycling, repurposing and mending) and counter-culturalism with regards to personal appearance (embracing the 'authentic' aspects of bodily experience that mainstream beauty culture rejects: stretch marks, natural body hair, unconventionally attractive body and face types, and so forth, as well as celebrating comfort over appearance).

Based on this list, one can see the potential appeal.

And the appeal is strong: the goblincore subreddit saw growth of 395 percent from July 2020 to July 2021, and Etsy reported a 695 percent increase in 'goblincore' searches in June 2021.

To whom, then, is this movement appealing?

Anyone interested in embracing the anti-consumerist, environmentalist values that the movement espouses, of course—but there is more.

The goblincore movement is known for its diversity, with a significant population of LGBTQI+ members—and a significant proportion of ADHD and/or autistic members as well.

Which really should come as no surprise. A movement that celebrates authenticity and active nurturing of the parts of nature the mainstream rejects? A natural fit for those to whom mainstream society is also less than welcoming.

And much of the goblincore aesthetic can be considered ADHD in disguise: comfort over conformity;

the socially expected routines of daily bodily maintenance as overly complex and unmanageable; an affinity for wild places; attraction to (and distraction by!) small, shiny objects... In many ways, goblincore is inherently a movement representative of neurodivergence, of thinking in ways counter to mainstream ideologies, of connecting the dots differently and finding permission to be authentically oneself in doing so.

Small shiny things, green growing things, snakes and frogs and snails and that strong, take-your-breath-away emotional ache for things rejected by society... Yes. In this aesthetic can an ADHD heart take delight.

However.

While it is truly wonderful that such an aesthetic exists, there remains the troubling foundations on which its chosen mascot stands. Thus, throughout most of goblincore's existence, there has been significant pressure to rebrand this aesthetic—usually as 'crowcore' or 'crowpunk'—in order to avoid the anti-Semitic undertones of the goblin (exacerbated by goblincore proponents posting pictures of their collections of 'shinies' with tags such as 'greedy little goblin').

The elephant in the room then is this: to what extent is it ever possible to appropriate something once used as a tool of oppression and give it new meaning?

It is notable that scholarship on the topic of

linguistic reappropriation includes in the word's definition that it is the reclaiming of a historically oppressive, insulting or problematic word/phrase *initially by the group it was used to target*. By this definition, it would be impossible for non-Jewish people to 'reclaim' the word 'goblin' in order to define it as being *not* anti-Semitic. However, the case here is complex as 'goblin' has existed as a concept independent of anti-Semitism since its inception—if, and only if, we can assume it origins to be free of racial stereotyping; if we can assume the invention of trolls, brownies, elves and like to likewise be free of racial implications.

My initial assertion was that goblins are symbolic of the darker impulses of human beings. If goblins can be considered a reflection of the ugly side of humanity, perhaps the ugliness is this: racism and hatred, the impulse to consider some human beings less than, and to dehumanise such that their murder becomes no longer problematic.

It is a quandary, then, that their most contemporary incarnation symbolises radical inclusion, celebrating diversity in neurology, sexuality and more by its very nature.

Of course, it is difficult to purport to being inclusively representative if one's inclusivity is not truly intersectional...

But that is an issue for an entirely different book.

CONCLUSION

THANK YOU FOR JOINING ME ON THIS (BY NO MEANS definitive) journey uncovering the symbolic meaning behind these popular mythological beings. I hope you've learned something useful, interesting, or thought-provoking, and that at least something in this collection of articles has made you smile, ask questions, or reconsider the way you think about the world.

If it has, I'd love to hear about it. You can contact me at www.amylaurens.com or on Instagram as @ByAmyLaurens.

And, if you've enjoyed this book, an honest review or star rating at the retailer of your choice is always gratefully appreciated—word of mouth is still the best way to sell books <3

Until next time,

Amy

SELECTED REFERENCES

Alexander, Skye. (2014). *Fairies: The Myths, Legends, Lore*. Adams Media. Great Britain.

Alexander, Skye. (2012). *Mermaids: The Myths, Legends, Lore*. Adams Media. Great Britain.

Barber, Paul. (1989). *Vampires, Burial and Death*. Yale University Press, USA.

Baring-Gould, Sabine. (1865). *The Book of Were-Wolves*. Project Gutenburg.

Briggs, Katharine M. (2002). *The Fairies in Tradition and Literature*. Taylor & Francis Ltd. Great Britain.

Hutton, Ronald. (2014). "The Making of the Early Modern British Fairy Tradition." *Historical Journal* 57(4):1135–57.

Lavers, Chris. (2009). *The Natural History of Unicorns*. Granta. Great Britain.

Laskow, Sarah. (2019). *The Very Short, Entirely True History of Unicorns*. Penguin Group. USA.

McCallum, Heather. (Nov 2016). "The Werewolf/ Vampire Dichotomy." *In The Footsteps Of Monsters*. Macaulay Eportfolio Community. Accessed at: [https://eportfolios.macaulay.cuny.edu/monsters/tag/werewolves/]

Stoker, Bram. (1897). *Dracula*. Archibald Constable and Company. UK.

IMAGE CREDITS

Anderson, Sophie Gengembre. (Unknown). *Take the Fair Face of Woman, and Gently Suspending, With Butterflies, Flowers, and Jewels Attending, Thus Your Fairy is Made of Most Beautiful Things.*

Batten, John D. (1890). Goblin illustration. From Jacobs, Joseph. (1890). English Fairy Tales.

de Moraine, R. (1864). *Le Vampire.* From: Féval, Paul-Henri-Corentin. (1864). *Les Tribunaux Secrets.* Paris: Boulanger et LeGrand. Vol. 2, p. 112.

Dürer, Albrecht. (1501/1504). *Saint George Killing the Dragon.*

Goltzius, Hendrik. (1589). *Lycaon transformed into a Wolf.*

Unknown artist. (Latter 2nd century BCE). *Nereid riding a sea-bull.*

Unknown artist. Unicorn wall painting in Apadana, Shush, Iran.

ABOUT THE AUTHOR

AMY LAURENS has published a variety of non-fiction works, including the *Inkprint Writers* series of books on theme and worldbuilding for writers; *How To Plan A Pinterest-Worthy Party Without Dying* for party-planning aspirants; and *The 32 Worst Mistakes People Make About Dogs* for anyone interested in learning more about dogs and people's mistaken attitudes toward them.

Amy has also published numerous other books, including the award-winning *Sanctuary* series (starting with *Where Shadows Rise*) about Edge's semi-accidental quest to save fairyland from evil shadows; the *Storm Foxes* series (starting with *A Fox Of Storms And Starlight*) about Mina's journey to save her family from storm foxes and depression; and the *Kaditeos* series (starting with *How Not To Acquire A Castle*), about Evil Overlord Mercury's attempts to acquire herself a castle and low-key take over the world. Her novella *Bones Of The Sea,* about carnivorous mist and creepy bones, won the 2021 Aurealis for Best Fantasy novella.

You can find all these and more at
www.amylaurens.com/books and
www.inkprintpress.com.

INKPRINT WRITERS

More fantastic non-fiction from award-winning author Amy Laurens! In print and ebook at all online retailers, and from www.InkprintPress.com.

How To Write Dogs: The 33 Worst Mistakes Writers Make When They Write About Dogs

How To Theme: Understanding and Analysing the Connection Between Theme and Story for Writers and Students

How To Create Cultures: How Climate Influences The Cultures You Create, A Reference For Writers, Gamers And Amateur Geographers!

How To Create Life: Invent Plant And Animal Species That Really Fit Your World, A Reference For Writers, Gamers And Amateur Geographers!

How To Map: Be Accurate And Add Conflict To Your Story, A Reference For Writers, Gamers And Amateur Geographers!

www.ingramcontent.com/pod-product-compliance
Lightning Source LLC
Chambersburg PA
CBHW031313060726
47590CB00003B/1196

* 9 7 8 1 9 2 2 4 3 4 3 9 5 *